When God is Silent, He is Still Here

Jannie Anderson Booker

Jannie Anderson Booker

ISBN 979-8-90417-447-7

To my Lord, Abba Father.

To my husband, children, grandchildren, mother, late father, and siblings. To my mentors and prayer warriors who have kept me before Abba Father.

Jannie Anderson Booker

CONTENTS

But God did listen! He paid attention to my prayer.

-Psalm 66:19 NLT

ACKNOWLEDGMENTS

I want to give honor to my Lord, Abba Father, for all that He has done in my life. I do not take any kingdom assignment lightly, for I count it as a privilege and an honor. To my late father, who is with The Lord. My father molded me into a daddy's girl, which helped me see Abba Father more deeply, leaning into Him for love and protection.

To my mother, whom I have always known to be a woman who loves God and her children. It is her walk and obedience to God that have brought me here, and that you are reading this book. As I see her walk with God, it has inspired me to do the same.

To my children and grandchildren, who are the apple of my eye. I continue to pray that they will reach past me in the Holy Spirit and hold on to Abba Father as He leads them.

To my husband for the time and space that he gives me to walk with Abba Father. I have learned a lot in our marriage, and I thank you for every lesson.

When God is Silent, He is Still Here

Encouraging and powerful, ***When God is Silent, He is Still Here*** highlights God's presence in silence and shows through scripture how we can push past the doubts and recognize His answers.

Given the uncertain times we are experiencing, **When God is Silent, He is Still Here** is inspirational and compelling, correlating scripture, personal experience, and wisdom to draw you closer to God through His silence. Emphasis will be placed on: God's silence, biblical figures' journeys in distress, questioning God, waiting it out, and His presence. All the chapters have been written according to scripture for your reference when you are walking in that specific area of your life. I have personally walked through many waiting seasons in my life, and giving up was my comfort. Although I knew Abba Father to be with me, I never allowed my soul to wait in Him. The comfort I sought was to alleviate the pain of my flesh, and not the stretching of my faith by Abba Father.

I wrote this book drawing on wisdom and patience gained through prayer and His Word. This book highlights the times when God was silent yet still present for His people. This book is God-ordained because we have all faced times when we needed a Word from the Lord or confirmation of an answer. So, what better way to be encouraged than by looking at a great cloud of witnesses who have faced the same times we often find ourselves in? For many of you, the answer is already given but not yet realized. For others, you must wait for the manifestation of God's answer; and that is okay.

Waiting for the manifestation can be discouraging, but the key is to wait in Abba Father through your soul. I refer to the soul because many saints want to wait on Him, but flesh will never allow it. I believe it is when you are in your waiting season that you become discouraged and lose hope. Proverbs 13:12 declares, "hope deferred makes the heart sick, but a longing fulfilled is a tree of life" (NIV). Waiting for God's voice while discouraged, or waiting in the flesh, creates doubt that He is with you.

I want to remind you that you are a spirit being, and human intellect should never supersede the Wisdom of God. Your flesh may ask, 'Abba, can you hear me?' but there is nothing concerning you that Abba Father has not already answered. Even when He is silent, rest assured that His answer has already been given to you. I believe The Lord allows His silence to pull you into communion with Him. Silence is the place where your soul rejoices in the Lord, and you find strength.

In your quiet moments, I want you to remember that you are kingdom and your prayers are heard. Not only are you kingdom, but you are a son or a daughter of The Most High God. If you are on this earth, you will always need to be encouraged by hearing the Word of God. The Lord declared in Isaiah 65:24; "Before they call I will answer; while they are still speaking I will hear" (ESV). I know this scripture brings hope to you, for there is no other way to receive such a declaration from your Heavenly Father.

Embrace scriptural passages of believers who have faced doubt and periods of silence. The passages will prove to you that God is still here, despite how it feels. I have prayed to Abba Father that as you read and hear these words, you will know that God is with you. God will never forget you because He loves you, and you are important to Him. In God's silence, I want you to be encouraged and declare scriptures over yourself.

Doubt may come, but if doubt sets in your heart, declare Psalm 66:19; "But God did listen! He paid attention to my prayer" (NLT). God's silence should not feel like abandonment, but feel like a secret place where He speaks expressively to your soul. Sometimes God answers with an audible voice, and other times He confirms with His presence. It is God's sovereignty ways in how He chooses to speak, because it is for His glory. God's glory is not limited; it is carried in His presence, His audible voice, as well as His silence.

You must be confident of God's glory, because that is where His answers reside. His glory has spoken long before the creation of man, and He knows what He is doing. God is not bound to your way of communication; so, you must submit to His perfect ways. God's ways are higher than yours, and you cannot fully understand how He communicates unless you submit your heart to Him.

Submitting your heart to God is the best way to receive His answer. Because, without a submissive heart, reasoning His answer will leave you confused and doubtful. I do not believe your human mind can withstand all of God's ways of communication. God knows how to answer you, and if He chooses to show up rather than use His audible voice, He will do so. In this book, I use Abba Father, God, Him, Holy Spirit, and Jesus Christ interchangeably, but I am referring to the same Godhead in Colossians 2:9.

Chapter 1

When God is Silent

> *O God, do not be silent! Do not be deaf. Do not be quiet, O God.*
>
> *-Psalm 83:1*

As humans, we expect communication and seek it throughout the day for guidance. Communication from our Heavenly Father is just as important to the body of believers. If we do not hear from God, we may assume He is being silent and start to rationalize that God is absent. Flesh may perceive God is absent, but our spirit knows that God can never leave us. Isaiah 49:15 says, "Can a mother forget the baby...Though she may forget, I will not forget you!" (NIV). This is the good news, and the confidence our spirit relies on that God is always with us.

I believe God's silence is a suitable time for you to be silent as well. Not silent spiritually, but naturally, because silence allows your other senses to discern what God is doing through the Holy Spirit. Lamentations 3:28 says "Let him sit alone in silence, for the Lord has laid it on him" (NIV). Embrace silence with wisdom and trust God with the outcome. Moments of silence with The Lord will produce patience and increase faith in Him.

Patience requires wisdom, and it is evaluated at different times in your life. No one is exempt from their patience being tested; this journey we all must take. Now, faith is something we automatically have, but the level of faith determines how we trust. Submitting to God's will for our life helps our level of faith to increase.

As we go through the patience and faith test, it is imperative that we remember that God will answer. Abba Father will answer in His timing, and in His way, and it may not be audible. When we feel God is not audible, we should sit in silence so our spirit can receive His answer. The posture of sitting silently displays our humility to The Father, and His will for our lives. Kathryn Kuhlman said, "Hundreds have been healed just sitting quietly in the audience without any demonstration whatsoever... not even a sermon is preached... not even a song has been sung" (Liardon, 2003, p. 271).

Kathryn Kuhlman exemplified patience and trust in Abba Father when He was silent during church services. I believe her trust caused her faith to grow, and her heart welcomed His presence. Abba Father answers may not come how we expect, so our hearts must stay postured towards Him. When our hearts are postured with Abba Father, we will resonate with His presence and His silence. Like Kathryn Kuhlman, be content with how The Lord chooses to respond to your prayers.

God will answer you at unexpected times, and unexpected ways. He may answer with a powerful sense of urgency, or confirmation in your spirit. Those answers may come from a scripture, billboard, dream, or through communication with a friend. Regardless of the mode Abba Father chooses to communicate, be open to receive. What may be perceived as silence is God working; let us examine His servant, Job.

Job Chapter 40 - God Speaks Twice

The LORD said to Job: "Will the one who contends with the Almighty correct him? Let him who accuses

God answer him!" Then Job answered the LORD: "I am unworthy how can I reply to you? I put my hand over my mouth. I spoke once, but I have no answer twice, but I will say no more." [6] Then the LORD spoke to Job out of the storm: "Brace yourself like a man; I will question you, and you shall answer me. "Would you discredit my justice? Would you condemn me to justify yourself? Do you have an arm like God's, and can your voice thunder like his? (Job 40:1-9, NIV)

The Lord was silent in Job's complaints, and his friends' accusations. Job thought God was silent and has left him to perish in his sufferings. But the passage says that Abba Father spoke to Job out of the storm. God sees your storm, He hears your prayers, and He is still here. I believe God chooses the right moment when He has our full attention so we will not doubt Him.

All throughout the Bible we have great details on patriarchs seeking the Lord for answers. We do not know how, when, and where God will speak to us; but we are confident why He will answer us. God's message shows that He loves and cares about us. God is always with us even in

His perceived silence. "Messages are transmitted and received through silence; therefore, it is important not to misunderstand the role of silence in religious traditions" (Gutiérrez and Paniagua, 2024).

I misunderstood God's silence when I was praying and seeking God for a topic for my Masters' Theological Essay. A week had gone by, and there was still no answer to my prayers. I reminded God of the deadline, and that He has yet to answer me. In my moment of desperation, I hinted that Abba Father was silent. Instantly, it hit me that God had responded, but I had missed the answer.

I felt strongly in my spirit, 'in the silence He is still speaking.' I realized that Abba Father answered me silently, and He used His spirit to get my attention. I knew The Lord wanted my topic to focus on His silence and presence. Embracing His silence required patience, and quiet moments with The Lord. This book was birthed out of my own personal experience with God's silence.

Chapter 2

A Journey Through Time

> *"Go in peace,"* the priest replied. *"For the LORD is watching over your journey."*
>
> *-Judges 18:6*

Let's look at the journeys of others in the Bible who believed God was silent, yet He was still a very present help. As we dive into more passages, it is my prayer that you will be encouraged to know that God is still with you. If you have been praying and have not received the answers from God, remember He is still at work. Abba Father has answered you with His presence. Sit quietly or "be still and know that He is God" (Psalm 46:10).

1 Samuel Chapter 1 - Hannah's prayer

"Because the LORD had closed Hannah's womb, her rival kept provoking her in order to irritate her. This went on year after year. Whenever Hannah went up to the house of the LORD, her rival provoked her till she wept and would not eat. In her deep anguish, Hannah prayed to the LORD, weeping bitterly. And she made a vow, saying, "LORD Almighty, if you will only look on your servant's misery and remember me, and not forget your servant but give her a son, then I will give him to the LORD for all the days of his life, and no razor will ever be used on his head." So, in the course of time Hannah became pregnant and gave birth to a son. She named him Samuel, saying, "Because I asked the LORD for him. (1 Samuel 1:6-7, 10-11, 20, NIV)

These passages were selected to help you step into the shoes of Hannah. The Bible says she was provoked year after year because The Lord closed her womb. Imagine the heaviness Hannah carried as she journeyed to the house of God. She had to set her face a flint, encourage herself, and believe that this year God will answer by opening her womb.

It was in Hannah's darkest moments that she sought The Lord wholeheartedly and saw His need. Her prayers shifted from asking for a son to using me for your glory. Scripture noted this change with her deep anguish and vow to The Lord. God never left Hannah; He was waiting to answer her prayer. God needed Hannah's focus to shift to Him so that her prayers would establish the Kingdom.

We see God silent in Hannah's grief, but He answered through her spoken vow. I do not want you to misconstrue grief because there is a reward. Just like Hannah, God has an appointed time for your answer. When everything comes to fruition, you too will emphasize "Because I asked the Lord..." God cannot forget about you, and your prayers are not in vain.

Daniel Chapter 10 - Daniel's Visitation

...a revelation was given to Daniel. Its message was true and it concerned a great war. At that time I, Daniel, mourned for three weeks. So I was left alone, gazing at this great vision; I had no strength left, my face turned deathly pale and I was helpless. He said, "Daniel, you who are highly esteemed, consider carefully the words I am about to speak to you, and stand up, for I have now been sent to you." Then he continued, "Do not be afraid, Daniel.

Since the first day that you set your mind to gain understanding and to humble yourself before your God, your words were heard, and I have come in response to them. But the prince of the Persian kingdom resisted me twenty-one days. (Daniel 10:1-2, 8, 11, 23-23, NIV)

I want you to envision your moments of consecrating, fasting, and praying concerning a situation. In any of those moments, did you feel like the Lord forgot what He said? The book of Daniel describes his personal vision of a war he did not understand. Daniel went to his secret place at the river to inquire of the Lord. Just like Daniel, we too must get away from distractions and inquire of The Lord.

The vision came after Daniel had fasted 21 days. Daniel fasted because he had the prophetic word of God; he was contending with it. You, too, have the Word of God concerning you, and He expects you to stand on it. Isaiah 43:26 says, "review the past for me, let us argue the matter together, state the case…" (NIV). When we approach God, He is looking for His Word and His promises.

In moments of silence, do not forget the God that you serve. "God desires His leaders not to strive for Him in fearful, nervous energy, but to walk with Him in restful spiritual peace" (Damazio, 1988, p. 177). Daniel's fasting and praying were to humble himself and gain understanding. Again, we do not know the appointed time for our answers, but we know God is with us until He answers. In verse thirteen, the angel of God emphasized: *"the prince of the Persian kingdom resisted me twenty-one days."*

I believe this confession from the angel encouraged Daniel that silence does not mean absenteeism. As the body of Christ, we can get discouraged when God is silent and our prayers seem to be delayed. I want to encourage you that when you pray, God hears you and has already answered you. If the answer seems delayed, it could be that the angels of God are fighting on your behalf. Paraphrasing Paul in Ephesians 6:12, we wrestle not with flesh and blood, but against forces of evil in the heavenly realms.

Luke Chapter 2 - Anna Bears Witness

'There was also a prophet, Anna, the daughter of Penuel, of the tribe of Asher. She was very old; she had lived with her husband seven years after her marriage and then was a widow until she was eighty-four. She never left the temple but worshiped night and day, fasting and praying. Coming up to them at that very moment, she gave thanks to God and spoke about the child to all who were looking forward to the redemption of Jerusalem. (Luke 2:36-38, NIV)

In these passages, we see Anna, the prophetess continuing the will of God while she waited for her Redeemer. The Bible specifically notes that Anna was old and a widow. In biblical days, it was hard for widows to sustain themselves, but we see that Abba Father cared for Anna's needs. Anna did not allow silence, nor difficult seasons to deter her kingdom assignment. Anna continued to fast and pray in the temple of God until the coming of the Messiah.

When the time came, Anna rejoiced when Mary and Joseph presented Jesus Christ to her. Anna continued her joy by telling everyone that the Redeemer had finally come. There will be times when you must wait while fasting and praying. Just like Anna the prophetess, your conduct must be consistent with your beliefs. Verse 37 emphasize *"She never left the temple but worshiped night and day, fasting and praying."*

When you face prolonged periods of waiting, your conduct should exemplify hope and consistency. When you are consistent in your walk before God, you show trust in His omnipotent and omniscient power. During all seasons of your life, your character should display Jesus Christ. When you display Christ, others will see that the Lord is with you. Those that looked upon Anna knew she was a woman of God and also believed she would live to see her Redeemer.

Anna the prophetess lived her life according to 2 Corinthians 6:3, "We put no stumbling block in anyone's path, so that our ministry will not be discredited" (NIV). When Anna opened her mouth, they heard wisdom and edification. Anna the prophetess was obedient to the Gospel she lived by, while awaiting the Lord's timing. There is no account in Anna's life that she doubted The Father's presence, or His ability to hear in those 84 years of silence. Silence can become overwhelming, but remember God hears, and is with you.

Chapter 3

Abba Father, Can You Hear Me?

> *O you who hear prayer, to you shall all flesh come.*
>
> *-Psalm 65:2*

I encourage you to be open to Abba Father's way of communication, so you will not miss His answers. Get this deep in your spirit; Abba Father hears you and has sent His answer to you. Job 33:13-14 says, "Why do you complain to him that he responds to no one's words? For God does speak now one way, now another though no one perceives it" (NIV). Moving forward, agree with God's Word through daily declarations and be vigilant to the enemy's plot to discourage you into silence.

The enemy knows that if he can silence you spiritually, then naturally, you will believe God does not hear you. Also, if the enemy can get you discouraged, then you will believe God is not with you. I know this all too well because the enemy once silenced me. He was very subtle and manipulative in this warfare against me. In that time of warfare, I did not realize that God was working on me.

With all the pounding and accusations coming against me, I shut down. I said, "Lord you know, and I am tired." I was worn out physically and mentally from the trial, and I did not want to engage in spiritual battle anymore. I concurred with Psalm 119:81, "I am worn out waiting for your rescue, but I have put my hope in your word" (NLT). That was a hard season, but I knew deeply that Abba Father was developing patience within me.

When God is processing us and developing patience within us, the enemy looks for direct access through our flesh. The enemy's strategy is to overwhelm the flesh because this is where he operates to silence your spirit. Naturally, the flesh does not want to be disturbed, as it seeks to stay balanced. But if we do not put on the full armor of God, the enemy will work the flesh to his advantage. If the enemy can weigh us down, our spirit will follow suit, leaving us spiritually silent.

It is safe to become silent in trials while trusting Abba Father, but it is never safe to use that silence as an occasion against God. If you are not listening to God in your silence, you can spiritually shut down. If you shut down spiritually, the enemy will use that time to draw you from God. Distancing us from God is the enemy's goal for the body of Christ. The enemy starts by whispering lies that God does not hear us, hoping we will believe them.

Becoming silent in warfare is strategic; you must understand how to conduct silent warfare. Job 33:31 says, "Pay attention, Job, and listen to me; be silent, and I will speak" (NIV). God speaks through His spirit, and that response can take many forms. To receive His answer, the Spirit and not your flesh must lead you. If you allow flesh to lead, it will sabotage the work and the patience that is developing within you.

You must remain vigilant to the voice of God, whether it is audible or perceived as silent. Hearing Abba Father's voice comes with a great mandate for His children. Jesus Christ says, "My sheep listen to my voice; I know them, and they follow me" (John 10:27, NIV). This scripture is key to listening and moving in obedience when in silent warfare. Following God's voice will keep you from deception and the snares of the enemy.

Obedience to God in silent warfare is also crucial because the enemy will begin to speak loudly and contrary to God's will. Satan will speak thoughts like, 'God has left you,' and 'God will not answer you.' These thoughts are contrary to the cross and an enemy to Jesus Christ. We must take bold stances and declare, 'I will trust God even if I cannot see Him working.' Like the servant Job, we must discern that God is doing something within us.

Job Chapter 23 - Job Understands the Tests

But he knows the way that I take; when he has tested me, I will come forth as gold. My feet have closely followed his steps; I have kept to his way without turning aside. I have not departed from the commands of his lips; I have treasured the words of his mouth more than my daily bread. "But he stands alone, and who can oppose him? He does whatever he pleases. (Job 23:10-13, NIV)

Learning of Job's trials and my own experiences have pushed me to become a prophetic prayer warrior. I can say my battles were overwhelming, and the heat was turned up. My only recourse was to pray prophetically, knowing that Abba Father hears me. "Prophetic prayer will bring our future to us...we will begin to see the will of God being done..." (Bismark, 2012, p. 73). Even when I felt like God was not listening, there was no substitute for prayer.

It was either I pray prophetically or die spiritually, and death is not allowed in Christ Jesus. Paraphrasing Peter to Jesus, who shall we go to? You have the words of eternal life (John 6:68). I prayed Abba Father's Word until His response manifested in my life. There were many days and nights I could not utter a word, but the Holy Spirit was my helper. I moaned and travailed until the words came up prophetically out of my belly.

The words that you speak over yourself have power, and you should only speak what God says prophetically. It is easy to be like the servant Job and accuse God, but that mindset does not resolve the affliction. It is how you submit to His will and His process for your life that will determine your victory. Not only does God hear your prayers, but He also hears your complaints against Him and your situation. God will not love you any less for complaining, but your complaints can distort how you hear from Abba Father.

Abba Father speaks expressively, and He knows how to get His message to you. How God decides to speak is His sovereignty, but it is your mandate to believe. Throughout God's Word, we see His promises to us. Isaiah 59:1 says, "Surely the arm of the LORD is not too short to save, nor his ear too dull to hear" (NIV). To reiterate, Abba Father can hear your prayers and is with you to help you.

I believe most of our questions and doubts arise when God is silent in His response. These feelings are natural because we want to know if He can hear us. God, in all His magnificent power, continues to show us why we should believe Him. "Studies have shown that nonverbal messages are generally more believable than verbal ones; when verbal and nonverbal messages contradict one another, most people believe the nonverbal" (Fontenot, 2023). As we grow closer to God, we will listen through what we see; even when we do not hear Him audible.

Genesis Chapter 4 – Abel's Blood Answered

And in the process of time, it came to pass that Cain brought of the fruit of the ground an offering unto the LORD. And Abel, he also brought of the firstlings of his flock and of the fat thereof. And the

LORD had respect unto Abel and to his offering: But unto Cain and to his offering he had not respect. And Cain was very wroth, and his countenance fell. And Cain talked with Abel his brother: and it came to pass, when they were in the field, that Cain rose against Abel his brother, and slew him. And the LORD said unto Cain, Where is Abel thy brother? And he said, I know not: Am I my brother's keeper? And he said, What hast thou done? the voice of thy brother's blood crieth unto me from the ground. (Genesis 4:3-5, 8-10, KJV)

Abel did not do anything to provoke his death. Abel was slain by his brother Cain because he gave his best to Abba Father. Cain was angry with God and projected his anger onto his brother, Abel. There will be times when we are wronged because of what God spoke over us, and this is expected as children of God. Continue to do God's will, pray for your enemy, and Abba Father will respond on your behalf.

I believe our heart posture plays a significant role in how and when God answers. Abba Father's answer is not provoked solely by our actions. But He does call for the heart to respond. 1 Chronicles 22:19 says, "Now devote your heart and soul to seeking the Lord your God..." (NIV). Whatever The Lord has called us to do, we must do it regardless of our trials.

The more intense the trial, the more we cry out for relief. Sometimes those trials have lasted a long time and have violated our peace. I remember standing in my bathroom with something heavy on my heart and I began to say, "Lord I have no words but hear my heart." I believe there are moments in our life where our hearts pray for us. If we have a heart postured toward God, it can intercede for us.

With a sincere heart, we can be confident that God has heard us even when He gives a silent answer. God controls a sincere heart that seeks to only do His will. Even if we do not give full control to Abba Father, He is still sovereign to do His will. Scripture says, "the king's heart is in the hand of the Lord, as the rivers of water: he turneth it whithersoever he will" (Proverbs 21:1, KJV). When you give Abba Father full control of our heart, you will then understand that He hears and answers.

Chapter 4

Wait It Out

> *I wait for the LORD, my soul waits, and in his word I hope.*
>
> -Psalm 130:5

In the waiting, we get discouraged and want to give up, even though we know God's Word and His will for our lives. The wait can naturally feel like crushing because the flesh is no longer satisfied. Flesh will never wait and never submit; so, our soul must lead us into waiting. Waiting it out means we must wait in God, not wait on God. Waiting in God protects us from being consumed in the furnace while He develops us with patience.

God will use your waiting period to refine you as gold in the furnace. In the furnace God may be silent, but He is for you and hears you. When you do not hear God's audible voice, trust He is answering you by fire. Purification does not sound like an answer from God, because it feels like tribulation in the flesh. The Bible often refers to the skin as flesh, which is the body's first line of defense naturally.

Flesh is the first to respond to discomfort, and it signals distress every time we are waiting on God. But when we are waiting in God, our soul leads and responds with quietness. Our soul embraces God's answers for us because our soul was made alive with His breath. Flesh has no trust in waiting, but our soul trusts through divine connection to Abba Father. As we wait in God for answers, we should profess hope, as King David did in the book of Psalms.

Psalm Chapter 62 - King David's Wait

> Let all that I am wait quietly before God, for my hope is in him. He alone is my rock and my salvation, my fortress where I will not be shaken. My victory and honor come from God alone. He is my refuge, a rock where no enemy can reach me. O my people, trust in him at all times. Pour out your heart to him, for God is our refuge. Interlude. (Psalm 62:5-8, NLT)

King David spent many decades waiting for God, overcoming battles, and trusting God to hear his prayers.

King David won every war, but in some battles, he felt discouraged and defeated. The times when King David's flesh led him were when he was grieved. Every time King David felt weak and unheard, he encouraged himself and remembered his help. Scripture tells us, "...But David found strength in the Lord his God" (1 Samuel 30:6, NIV).

As you wait in God, remember that you will never be left alone to figure it out. God is always with you, but you must be open to the way He responds. God's response may be in the furnace, in battles, or silently, but remember He hears and answers. If you feel like your battles are overwhelming, and waiting in God is too much, remember King David. For 40 years, King David reigned and wrote many poems about waiting it out.

You may be more uncomfortable with the waiting process than with the trials. We have been conditioned to declare victory in warfare, but the waiting may leave us in doubt. I believe it leaves us in doubt because it is not our hands but the hand of God that is orchestrating the test. Since it is God that is developing us, we should rest assured that He is with us. The book of James tells us why we deal with trouble and the purpose of waiting it out.

James Chapter 1 - Wait for Endurance

Dear brothers and sisters, when troubles of any kind come your way, consider it an opportunity for great joy. For you know that when your faith is tested, your endurance has a chance to grow. So let it grow, for when your endurance is fully developed, you will be perfect and complete, needing nothing. (James 1:2-4, NLT)

Waiting helps you rely completely on God, the author and finisher of your faith. Abba Father knows the amount of trouble that will push you closer to Him. The closer you are to Abba Father, the better you can hear Him and wait patiently. It is not God's desire to send trouble that will cause you to run from Him. The goal is for you to have everything you need in Him and to love Him with all of your heart.

I declare we are a body of believers that wait effectively; and we give no place to the enemy. I declare we are an effective witness to someone else. I declare we will wait like King David and remain faithful in trials. Revelation 12:11, we overcome the enemy by the Blood of the Lamb and the words of our testimony. All testimonies should

Jannie Anderson Booker

reveal the Glory of God in our lives, and points everything back to Christ.

Chapter 5

He is Still Here

> *This is my command be strong and courageous!*
> *Do not be afraid or discouraged. For the LORD*
> *your God is with you wherever you go.*
>
> *-Joshua 1:9*

This final chapter emphasizes Abba Father's presence, and His plan to grow your faith. Can you think back to times when you prayed and it was answered immediately? I can remember my excitement for the quick results; I used to say, "God always answer my prayers." In my mind, I was in alignment with God because whenever I prayed Abba Father answered. What I did not realize at the time was that I was a babe in Christ, and my faith had not yet been tested.

I still needed to mature in my walk, but Abba Father graciously gave me quick answers to my prayers. As parents, we do the same for our children. When babies cry, we tend to them and run to their aid to give them comfort. However, once that baby becomes a toddler, we are not running as fast because we want them to engage in simple tasks. Once they start maturing into a teenager, we step back and let them grow up to make the right choices.

It is the same concept when you are matured in Christ. God may not answer immediately and that is okay because He is growing your faith. God's delay does not nullify His presence in your life; He is still here. If God answered every prayer immediately, we would never understand how He gives us choices to pursue. Deuteronomy 30:19 says, "... I have set before you life and death, blessings and curses. Now choose life, so that you and your children may live" (NIV).

I believe the delay in answers are stretching your faith and catapults you into a different dimension in Christ. Delayed answers help you to know Jesus Christ in the fellowship of His suffering. That fellowship matures you in the valley, in the wilderness, and on the mountaintop. It does not matter how long the season of delay is, because you are promised victory. Walk in every season of your life proclaiming Abba Father is still here just as the Israelites did.

Joshua Chapter 6 – God instructs Israel.

Then the LORD said to Joshua, "See, I have delivered Jericho into your hands, along with its king and its fighting men. March around the city once with all the armed men. Do this for six days. Have seven priests carry trumpets of rams' horns in front of the ark. On the seventh day, march around the city seven times, with the priests blowing the trumpets. When you hear them sound a long blast on the trumpets, have the whole army give a loud shout; then the wall of the city will collapse and the army will go up, everyone straight in." When the trumpets sounded, the army shouted, and at the sound of the trumpet, when the men gave a loud shout, the wall collapsed... (Joshua 6:2-5, 20, NIV)

The children of Israel supernaturally conquered Jericho by placing their faith in God and by believing He was with them. They marched around Jericho's wall for seven days by blowing the trumpet and giving a mighty shout on the seventh day. By faith, they heard from God, and their fellowship with Him caused them to march. When God was satisfied with their level of obedience and faith, the walls of

Jericho came down. Hebrews 11:30 says, "By faith the walls of Jericho fell, after the army had marched around them for seven days" (NIV).

Humanly, it was impossible for the brass sound of the trumpet, or their mighty shout to cause the bricks to crumble. The wall came down by the hand of the almighty God Himself. It was Abba Father moving at His own pace, own timing, and doing His own divine complete will. In that seven-day delay, Abba Father knew some hearts would be heavy, and their legs would be fatigued. Yet, Abba Father waited for complete surrender before He dismantled the walls of Jericho.

I believe God allowed the seven-day march because seven signifies completion and wholeness. When your faith is complete and whole, then you can rest in God to do the work. While God is working, continue to do what Abba Father has called you to do. You still have a responsibility to Abba Father to pray, so do not stop praying. 1 Peter 3:12 says, "For the eyes of the Lord are on the righteous and his ears are attentive to their prayer..." (NIV).

Remember how our God delivered the three Hebrew boys, Shadrach, Meshach, and Abednego from Nebuchadnezzar's fire? Scripture says that the furnace was turned seven times more than the normal custom. It does not matter how bad the situation is, Jesus Christ is with you. God is with you every season of your life. Psalm 34:17 says, "when his people pray for help, he listens and rescues them from their troubles" (CEV).

Christ Jesus knows all the things we will ever encounter and has equipped us with His Word. The Word of God reminds us of who we are, and Who we belong to. The Word will strengthen us and encourage us not to give in or bow down to this world. Trouble will always be with us, but trouble has no authority over us. Trouble should never speak louder than Abba Father because His Word should be our guidance.

God promised you in His word that He will not fail you, and you can count on Him to be there. Jeremiah 29:12-13 says, "Then you will call on me and come and pray to me, and I will listen to you. You will seek me and find me when you seek me with all your heart" (NIV). This scripture reminds me that any doubt that I have is a heart issue, and not a God issue. I may want God to hear me and be with me, but my heart must be in alignment to see that He is already with me.

Your heart is key in knowing God, and His will for your life. If your heart is not postured towards the Lord, then you will not realize His presence. The enemy loves to speak lies into your heart concerning your situation. The enemy will say you are going through this alone, and your mind may believe it. Paul said in 2 Corinthians 10:5, "Casting down imaginations, and every high thing that exalteth itself against the knowledge of God, and bringing into captivity every thought to the obedience of Christ" (KJV).

God is after your heart; when He has your heart, He knows the enemy cannot deceive you. You serve a God that will never leave you for your shortcomings. God is patient and will continue to tug on the heart to align it with Him. Everything you endure is for your personal walk with the Lord. Because the test is personal, God has an intimate reason to be present.

So many times, we go through testing and feel like God is not with us. God proved Himself to many patriarchs in the Bible who did not think He was with them. God planned for the children of Isreal's impossible situation to escape death in their own strength. The Red Sea was before the children of Israel, and Pharoh along with his army was behind them. But when God spoke to Moses to lift his staff over the Red Sea, they saw that God was with them.

Do not let trials stop you from advancing in The Lord. Abba Father wants you to continue moving forward regardless of the threats that surround you. Exodus 14:15 says, "Then the Lord said to Moses, "Why are you crying out to me? Tell the people to get moving!" (NLT). This scripture should confirm to your spirit that Abba Father is here and waiting for your obedience. Acknowledge what Abba Father tells you to do and take Him at His word.

Just as God has done throughout the Bible, He will continue to prove His presence and get the glory. Whatever seems impossible to you, is the area where Abba Father wants to grow your faith. Prophet Hosea tells us, "Let us acknowledge the Lord; let us press on to acknowledge him. As surely as the sun rises, he will appear; he will come to us like the winter rains, like the spring rains that water the earth" (Hosea 6:3, NIV). Keep moving forward, Abba Father is with you and leading you into victory.

Jannie Anderson Booker

Reflection

> *Giving the uncertain times we are experiencing, inspirational and compelling, **When God is Silent, He is Still Here** correlates scriptures, personal experience, and wisdom to draw you closer to God through His silence.*

Now that we have witnessed Abba Father at work, I want to leave you with some impactful thoughts on His sovereignty. When God is silent, He is still communicating with you through His spirit. Take some quiet time and sit with the Lord to allow Him to show you, His presence. Embrace moments of silence, knowing that the Lord is developing your patience and increasing your faith. It is important to note that all of God's children have navigated storms without God's audible voice.

Remember, God can never forget about you; it is His desire for you to trust and love Him. Yes, He hears you; but you must wait in God so that the processing does not overtake you. Be alert of the enemy's tactic to silence you and separate you from God. Abba Father desire is for you to remain close to Him in the storms. God will speak to you in the storm, but it will be His timing.

It is my prayer that this book has helped you embrace your waiting period in a new way. You are not just waiting for Abba Father; you are waiting in Him. As you wait in Him, allow your soul to lead you into purification. Flesh does not want to be disturbed so it will object to the move of God. The waiting process refines you, but it also helps you become a witness to someone else.

Congratulations! You now have the wisdom to embrace His silence in the valley, on the mountaintop, and in the wilderness. You know silence does not mean God is absent. You are equipped for every trial and know how to do silent warfare. Through faith you know God is with you and orchestrating your victory. Today, declare Abba Father is here even in His silence.

God Bless.

Notes

Bismark, ChiChi. (2012). Teach Us to Pray. Jabula
    Heights

Contemporary English Version. (1995). American Bible
    Society

Damazio, Frank. (1988). The Making of a Leader. City
    Bible Publishing

English Standard Version. (2025). Crossway. (Original
    work published 2001)

Fontenot, Karen. A. (2023). *Nonverbal Communication
    and Social Cognition.* EBSCO. Retrieved March
    30, 2026, from https://www.ebsco.com/research-
    starters/health-and-medicine/nonverbal-
    communication-and-social-cognition

King James Bible. (2020). Cambridge University Press.
    (Original work published 1769)

Liardon, Robert. (1996). God's Generals: Why They
    Succeeded and why Some Failed. God's General

López Gutiérrez, A. and Arroyo Paniagua, J. J. (2024). *An
    Exploration of Silence in Communication
    [Exploración del silencio en la comunicación].*

European Public & Social Innovation Review, 9, 01-18. https://doi.org/10.31637/epsir-2024-610

New Living Translation. (2015). Tyndale House Foundation. (Original work published 1996)

NIV, KJV, NASB, Amplified, Parallel Bible. (2020). Zondervan. (Original work published 1973/1960/1954)

Jannie Anderson Booker

About the Author

Evangelist Jannie Anderson Booker is Abba Father's daughter. She is a wife, mother, and grandmother. She is an anointed preacher, prophetess and prayer warrior. Evangelist Jannie faithfully served the Lord for over 21 years. Abba Father has entrusted Jannie with various areas of ministry, from preaching in the pulpit and conference speaking to evangelizing the streets. Evangelist Jannie holds no punches in ministry. She speaks with such boldness and passion to motivate believers, equip the Saints in prayer, and win souls for the Lord Jesus Christ. Evangelist Jannie's desire is for a mighty move of God and transformed lives through Jesus Christ and Holy Spirit. Jannie Booker is the founder of PSST Pure Simple Sincere True broadcast where life situations are conversed.